RESPECTING OTHERS

By Steffi Cavell-Clarke

Crabtree Publishing Company
www.crabtreebooks.com
1-800-387-7650

Published in Canada
Crabtree Publishing
616 Welland Avenue
St. Catharines, ON
L2M 5V6

Published in the United States
Crabtree Publishing
PMB 59051
350 Fifth Ave, 59th Floor
New York, NY 10118

Published by Crabtree Publishing Company in 2017

First Published by Book Life in 2016
Copyright © 2017 Book Life

Author
Steffi Cavell-Clarke

Editors
Grace Jones
Janine Deschenes

Design
Natalie Carr

Proofreader
Crystal Sikkens

Production coordinator and
prepress technician (interior)
Margaret Amy Salter

Prepress technician (covers)
Ken Wright

Print coordinator
Katherine Berti

Photographs
Stuart Monk/ Shutterstock: page 11
Other images by Shutterstock

Printed in Hong Kong/012017/BK20161024

Library and Archives Canada Cataloguing in Publication

Cavell-Clarke, Steffi, author
     Respecting others / Steffi Cavell-Clarke.

(Our values)
Issued in print and electronic formats.
ISBN 978-0-7787-3263-1 (hardback).--ISBN 978-0-7787-3329-4
(paperback).--ISBN 978-1-4271-1894-3 (html)

     1. Respect--Juvenile literature. 2. Respect for persons--
Juvenile literature. 3. Self-esteem--Juvenile literature. I. Title.

BJ1533.R4C38 2016   j179'.9   C2016-906660-6
                                            C2016-906945-1

Library of Congress Cataloging-in-Publication Data

Names: Cavell-Clarke, Steffi, author.
Title: Respecting others / Steffi Cavell-Clarke.
Description: New York : Crabtree Publishing Company, 2017. |
Series: Our
  values | Includes index.
Identifiers: LCCN 2016046766 (print) | LCCN 2016048584 (ebook) |
ISBN
  9780778732631 (hardcover : alk. paper) | ISBN 9780778733294 (pbk.
: alk.
  paper) | ISBN 9781427118943 (Electronic book text)
Subjects: LCSH: Respect for persons--Juvenile literature.
Classification: LCC BJ1533.R42 C38 2017 (print) | LCC BJ1533.R42
(ebook) |
  DDC 179/.9--dc23
LC record available at https://lccn.loc.gov/2016046766

CONTENTS

R0448550459

Words that are bolded, like **this**, can be found in the glossary on page 24.

WHAT ARE VALUES?

Values are the things that you believe are important, such as cooperating with others. The ways we think and behave depend on our values. Values teach us how we should **respect** each other and ourselves. Sharing the same values with others helps us work and live together in a **community**.

Respecting others

Working hard at school

Telling the truth

Values make our communities better places to live. Think about the values in your community. What is important to you and the people around you?

Respecting the law

Being responsible

Sharing your ideas

5

BEING RESPECTFUL

Being respectful means that we behave in a way that shows the people around us that we care about their feelings and rights. A right is something that every person is allowed to do or have, such as the right to go to school. We can be respectful by treating others the way we would like to be treated.

We can show respect toward other people by being polite, kind, and honest. People who show respect think about how their actions will affect others.

Danielle promises to walk her family dog every day after school. She shows respect to her family by following through on what she promised.

WHY IS RESPECT IMPORTANT?

Being respectful to each other allows us to work and live together happily within a community. It also allows us to build strong relationships with others by showing kindness toward them.

It is important to show each other respect because it means we care about other people's feelings. When we try to understand how others are feeling, we show them that we can be counted on and trusted. It is also important that other people respect our feelings, too.

How are you feeling?

Worried

Sad

Happy

Angry

RESPECTING THE LAW

Rules are instructions that teach us the right ways to behave. Laws are rules that are made by the **government**. People should always follow the laws in their community. Laws help keep us safe and help us make the right choices.

Laws include things such as not stealing or harming other people. We must not break the law. If we do, we are committing a **crime**.

Police officers

Police officers are people who help everyone in their communities. They have a very important job to do—they try to keep us safe from harm, and make sure that we all follow the law. It's important to show police officers the respect they show us.

11

RESPECTING OTHER BELIEFS

Choosing what to believe in is an important part of our **freedom**. Some people choose to follow the beliefs of a **religion**. There are many religions that people can choose to follow and they can be very different. We must always respect other people's beliefs, whether we agree with them or not.

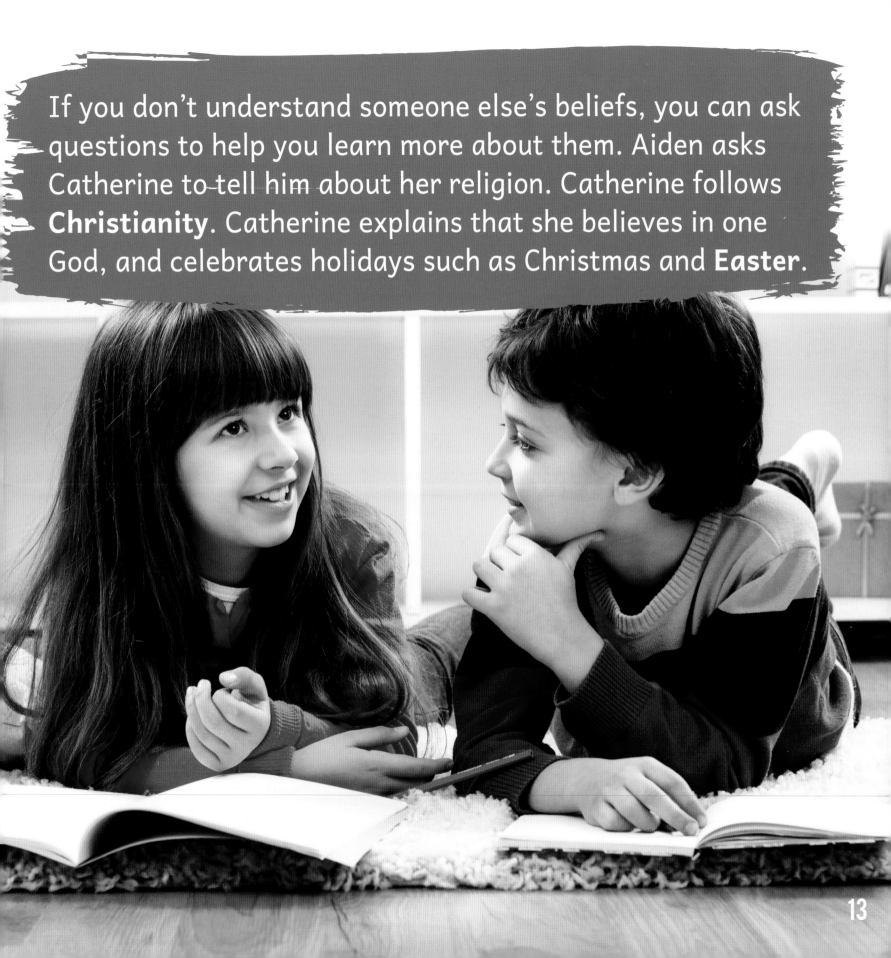

If you don't understand someone else's beliefs, you can ask questions to help you learn more about them. Aiden asks Catherine to tell him about her religion. Catherine follows **Christianity**. Catherine explains that she believes in one God, and celebrates holidays such as Christmas and **Easter**.

RESPECTING OURSELVES

It is very important that we respect ourselves. When we respect ourselves, we are showing self-respect. One way to show self-respect is to take care of our bodies by eating **nutritious** foods and exercising.

Another way to respect ourselves is to have good relationships with our friends and family. This means that we ask them to respect us, and we respect them in return.

Staying healthy and keeping clean also shows self-respect. Keeping clean is called **personal hygiene**. Sarah shows self-respect by brushing her teeth every morning.

LISTENING TO OTHERS

Listening to others is one way of showing respect toward them. It is important to listen to other people because it will help you understand what they might be thinking and how they might be feeling.

Thomas builds a strong relationship with his mother by showing her that he respects the things she says. He asks his mother how she is feeling because he cares about her. He listens to what she says and it makes them both feel happy and respected.

RESPECTING OTHERS AT SCHOOL

We must respect our teachers, classmates, coaches, parent volunteers, janitors, and others at school. Our teachers can teach us a lot of new things, so it is important that we are quiet when they are speaking and listen to them carefully.

Olivia follows the rules of the library whenever she visits. She is very quiet when people need to read without being **disrupted**. By being quiet, Olivia shows others that she respects them.

RESPECTING OTHERS AT HOME

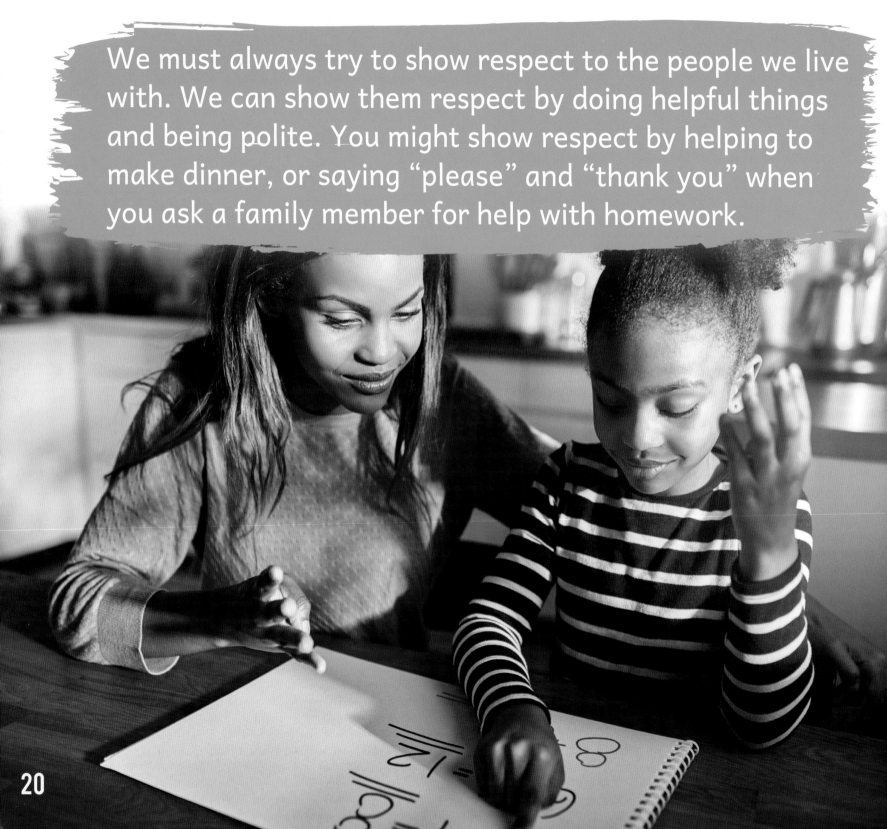

We must always try to show respect to the people we live with. We can show them respect by doing helpful things and being polite. You might show respect by helping to make dinner, or saying "please" and "thank you" when you ask a family member for help with homework.

Adam respects his parents and likes to help them with jobs around the house. He knows that making his bed and washing the dishes will help his parents, and show them that he cares about them.

21

MAKING A DIFFERENCE

We can respect the **environment** by putting our garbage in a garbage can. We can recycle paper, cardboard, and plastic so it can be reused, or made into new things.

Show respect for your community by never throwing litter on the ground.

Share

Think of all the ways you can show others that you respect them.

Be kind

Be helpful

Practice respect today and build strong relationships with everyone around you!

Say "hello"

Be polite

Listen

23

GLOSSARY

Christianity [kris-chee-AN-i-tee] A religion whose followers believe in the teachings of Jesus Christ

community [kuh-MYOO-ni-tee] A group of people who live, work, and play in a place

crime [krahym] An action that breaks the law

disrupted [dis-RUHPT-ed] To interrupt or disturb something

Easter [EE-ster] A Christian holiday that celebrates Jesus Christ

environment [en-VAHY-ruh n muh nt] Your surroundings

freedom [FREE-duh m] Being allowed to do something

government [guhv-ern-muh-nt] A group of people that run and make the laws for a certain area or place

nutritious [noo-trish-uh-s] Having substances that people need to be healthy

personal hygiene [PUR-suh-nl HAHY-jeen] Keeping yourself clean

religion [ri-LIJ-uh n] A set of values and beliefs that people follow

respect [ri-SPEKT] The act of giving something or someone the attention it deserves

responsible [ri-spon-suh-buhl] Reliable or dependable

INDEX